Hugs, Handshakes & High Fives

Written By
David Schon and
Casey Pilar

Illustrations by
Marcela Ribero

ISBN: 1453698795
ISBN-13: 9781453698792

Once upon a time, there was a boy named Travis. Travis was born into this world with powers of the greatest kind.

Travis's powers included never fussing, hardly ever causing trouble for his parents, and most importantly, the power to change the world!

While Travis always tried to *see the good* in the world and think positive thoughts, and his laugh and fun-loving smile could cheer up a large room, one thing stood in his way – he was born with special needs.

Travis didn't look, walk or talk like other kids. Sometimes, he would fall because of balance problems, or he would get frustrated because he couldn't get his mouth to form the right words – so he sometimes had trouble talking.

Some people were scared when he was around because they didn't know that in his heart, he was just like everyone else.

They would turn their heads away
when they saw him or make a
point to avoid walking past him.

The awful ways that strangers acted hurt Travis's feelings.
He felt that just because he looked, walked and talked a little
differently than they did, didn't mean that he was a bad kid,
or that he didn't deserve the same friendly smile or greeting
as everyone else.

What was wrong with these people?
There are many people in the world that are different.

Some people are in wheelchairs,
speak a different language or are of a different culture.
There are many things that make us all unique.

Travis knew that all
of these people had
abilities and talents,
too, just like he did.
He knew that he had
to make a difference.

Travis tried to look back kindly at people who were staring at him, or he would walk closer to people who looked scared. None of this seemed to make a difference.

He then tried to get all of his friends together and come up with better ways to teach people about their mistreatments.

This didn't work either.

Suddenly, Travis had a big, new idea! Hugs, handshakes and high fives! He was going to make sure to give out as many of these hugs, handshakes and high fives as he possibly could!

He would look directly at those who looked down on him and offer his greatest powers – the ability to show others how he is no different than them and maybe even a little better!

The next day, his first stop to try out his new idea was the mall.

He spent hours making people laugh and have fun.
It was working – really working!

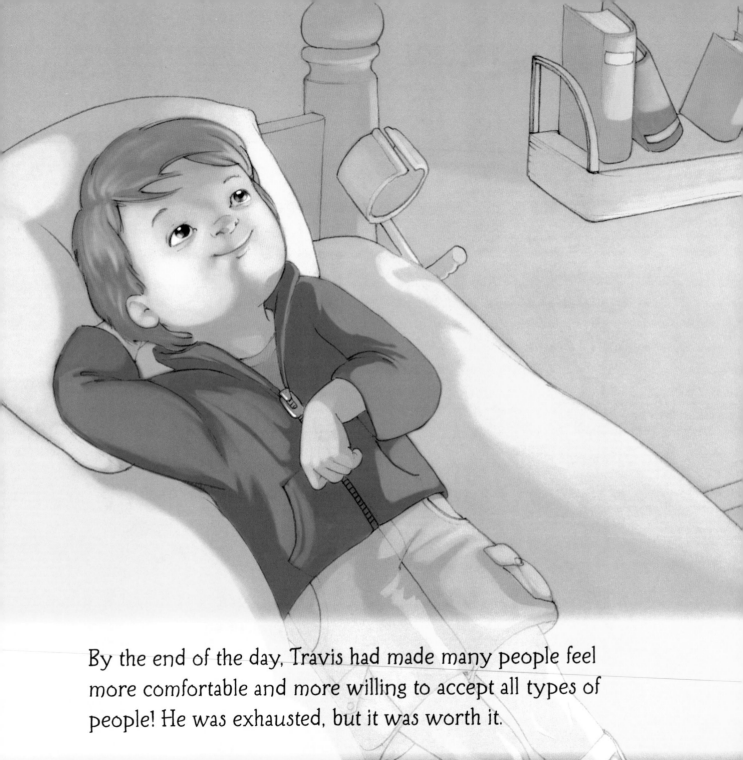

By the end of the day, Travis had made many people feel more comfortable and more willing to accept all types of people! He was exhausted, but it was worth it.

As Travis got ready for bed that night, he realized what he was able to do in just one day. He thought he could do more, though. He wanted EVERYONE to offer hugs, handshakes, and high fives to all of the special people around them.

So, Travis closed his eyes, raised his hands and chanted: "HUGS, HANDSHAKES and HIGH FIVES! HUGS, HANDSHAKES, and HIGH FIVES!" POOF!

When he opened his eyes, he knew that something had changed.

When he got up the next day, he saw that he was right!

Everywhere he went, people were giving hugs, handshakes
and high fives, and everyone was happy and smiling.

What a wonderful place the world had become, and
it was all because of Travis! Travis changed the world
with his hugs, handshakes and high fives!!

You, too, can help Travis change the world! When you are out in public, at a soccer game or the mall or just about anywhere, don't be afraid to offer a high five to someone with special needs, or introduce yourself and give out a handshake like you would with any new friend. Better yet, when you get to know someone with special needs, give them a hug just like you do with other friends in your life.

The Alexander Foundation is determined to get the message out that people with special needs are like everyone else; they need acceptance, gratitude, love and affection. They need to be included in everyday events and need to be treated like everyday people. By reading this book to your children, and discussing the difference you and they can make with the treatment of people with special needs, you will help pass on a very important message. We all deserve a place in this great world, and we all deserve equal respect, attention and the right to be as one.

Thank you from your friends at the Alexander Foundation.

www.TheAlexanderFD.org